GW01079897

JABEZ

A LITTLE BOOK
OF BIG BLESSINGS!

By

CATHERINE BROWN

Published by

The Transparent Publishing Company

www.TransparentPublishing.co.uk

Paperback ISBN 978-1-909805-24-8
eBook ISBN 978-1-909805-27-9

First published September 2015

Original Copyright holder - Catherine Brown

Cover Photography by Peter Ribbeck

www.PeterRibbeck.com

Unless otherwise stated all Scriptures quoted are from New International Version

CONTENTS

INTRODUCTION

THE PRAYER OF JABEZ (KJV)

And Jabez called on the God of Israel, saying,
"Oh that thou wouldest bless me indeed,
And enlarge my coast
And that thine hand might be with me,
And that thou wouldest keep me from evil,
That it may not grieve me.
And God granted him that which he requested." KJV 1 Chronicles
4:10

THE PRAYER OF JABEZ (NIV)

"Jabez cried out to the God of Israel,
Oh, that you would bless me
And enlarge my territory!
Let your hand be with me,
And keep me from harm
So that I will be free from pain.
And God granted his request."

NIV 1 Chronicles 4:10

Genealogy/background

It is widely thought that Jazeb belonged to the tribe of Judah and eventually became the notable head of a clan. Ezra, the Chronicler, is writing about Jabez in a post exilic era. It is implied that Jabez was well known since Ezra does not take time to introduce him.

Many Jews consider Jabez to be a famous doctor of the law who left numerous disciples behind him. The bible tells us that families of the scribes dwelt at Jabez, *"And the clans of scribes who lived at Jabez:"* 1 Chronicles 2:55a

Albeit the pages of history seem to point to a notable man who left a wonderful legacy for his family, when we first meet Jabez in the pages of Chronicles we cannot say with certainty whether he was famous or unknown. What we can be sure of is that he had a difficult beginning; the name his mother gave him bears witness to that. Ultimately he prayed an extremely unusual, short prayer that God answered in a remarkable way and Jabez became an abundantly blessed man. The prayer of Jabez is not a magic formula, nor a mantra to be repeated in the vain hope of some positive response from God. However, there are certain Kingdom principles contained within it that are keys with which we might unlock untold blessings and miracles in our own lives.

There are eight essential points we can quickly take note of from the prayer of Jabez:

1. Jabez was considered to be more honourable than his brothers
2. His birth and early life had been marked by pain and suffering even in his naming as a "man of sorrows"
3. He called on the God of Israel in prayer
4. He asked God to bless him
5. He asked God to enlarge/extend his territory/coast
6. He asked for God's hand to be with him
7. He asked God to keep him from harm/temptation
8. God answered his prayer!

From these eight points we can begin to apply our own faith to the firm foundation that we can see established in the life of Jabez, a man so graciously blessed by God.

CHAPTER 1

WHAT'S IN A NAME?

"Jabez was more honourable than his brothers. His mother had named him Jabez, saying "I gave birth to him in pain."
1 Chronicles 4:9

Why does the Chronicler record that Jabez was considered to be more honourable than his brothers? Perhaps it was because he had set his heart to please God no matter what he faced. One thing I have learned in life is that when trouble and trials assail us, to focus on the inherent goodness of God is crucial if we are to remain faith-filled, obedient to the Holy Spirit and rise not just somehow, but victorious above our circumstances.

Jabez excelled in virtue above his brothers. He was eminent in learning and renowned in piety. He was a man of prayer, devoted to God, trusting only in the God of Israel. He acknowledged God in all of his ways and this put him under divine blessing, favour and protection and He prospered under God. It's clear that in the time of his affliction he remembered to bless God and call upon His mighty name. *"Commit to the LORD whatever you do, and your plans will succeed." Proverbs 16:3*

What's in a Name?

The Hebrew word for Jabez means *'pain'* or *'man of sorrows'*. Why did Jabez' mother name him in such a way? The Chronicler notes that she gave birth to Jabez *"in pain."* We can legitimately say that pain is an aspect of all labour and the process of giving birth for every woman is painful, yet it is evident that the world is not full of children called *Jabez*; to the inquisitive mind this provokes further thought on the naming of the boy.

We all face painful circumstances at some point in our lives. What can we learn from the life of Jabez? What did he pray that shifted him from being a man of sorrows to a man who was exceptionally blessed? Can and will God do it again and do it for us?

The naming of a child points both to their past e.g. family heritage and also to their future potential. For instance, many families who name their first born child after a father or mother and/or grandfather/grandmother are seeking to honour previous generations. In ancient biblical times the choosing of a name was often the expression of aspiration and/or prophecy about a child's future. For instance *Solomon* means *'peaceful.'* Solomon succeeded his father King David and reigned over Israel as a man of peace. Whilst names can bring definition only God can fulfil destiny in our lives.

When naming our own children, my husband and I spent time in prayer and in the Scriptures searching for the names we believed God had in mind for each one of them. It was a precious and powerful time of seeking the mind of the Lord. We knew God had a special plan for each of them and we wanted their names to somehow reflect that God-given purpose.

When naming our son *Daniel*, we had a strong impression that he would become a young man of great intellect that God would use for His glory and that he would be a peer to his peers just like his namesake in the bible. Now as a young adult Daniel is living up to his God-given name; he is academically brilliant and he is clearly popular with his peers, and has the capacity to influence and lead just like his namesake.

As we look to the time of Jabez' birth it is clear that things were not easy in his household. We might ask what was it about this season of Jabez mother's life that caused her to name her son in such a negative manner? Was her pregnancy difficult? Did the boy's father abandon them? Did the father die? Was it a physically difficult birth? Were the family facing financial crisis? The truth is we will never know this side of Heaven why she named her son Jabez, but we can think compassionately about the woman's situation nonetheless.

When I gave birth to my daughter Rebecca, the anaesthetic failed to work and I had to endure the pain of a Caesarean without any pain relief initially. I know what it is to give birth in pain nonetheless my pain soon gave way to the joy of receiving the gift of a little girl from God.

It is useful to consider the circumstances surrounding the birth and early years of the young man Jabez who experienced an epiphany of such magnitude that he moved from a position of "pain" to "gain." In one magnificent faith-fuelled prayer it became a transformational point in his life and propelled him into what God our Father had prepared for him.

Our Past Should Not Define or Confine Us

One important lesson we can learn from the naming of Jabez and his subsequent prayer of faith is that no matter what circumstances we are born into (including any painful or traumatic situations our parents may have faced), every child of God is positioned in Christ to be an over-comer and to rise victoriously over their situations to the glory of God!

Our past or present difficulties are not to become a thing that will confine or define us and nor should pain become a roadblock on the path of destiny. Jabez knew God as deliverer of Israel and in God he placed a fervent hope as we may also choose to do today. Just like Jabez, every believer must elect to surrender their will to the goodness of God and trust Him as mighty Deliverer.

Moses cried out for God's people to give them proportionate gladness for sadness, *"Make us glad for as many days as you have afflicted us, for as many years as we have seen trouble." Psalm 90:15*

One thing I have learned of the goodness of God is that when He brings restoration, there is nothing missing; everything is restored at present day value. For every testimony birthed in tears God will produce a song of celebration in His perfect time.

I heard a quotation once that succinctly expresses something of this truth; *"When you are standing on the edge of a cliff, trust God, surrender and let go. He will either catch you when you fall or teach you how to fly!"* Man's extremities become God's opportunities to bless us!

Even in the midst of trials and troubles Jabez called out to God to bless him. May we be encouraged and aspire to live a simple life of faith that flows with the knowledge and manifestation of God's gracious blessing and goodness.

"Oh Lord, bless me indeed – for the glory of your Name and the expansion of your Kingdom,"

In Jesus name,
Amen

CHAPTER 2

BLESS ME O GOD

*"Jabez cried out to the God of Israel,
Oh, that you would bless me"*

Jabez was a man of God who refused to accept a negative word spoken over his life and instead demonstrates to us the power of appropriating God's blessing through the prayer of faith. It is ever my conviction that we can only multiply once we have a fruitful model to follow and the prayer of Jabez gives us one such pattern of increase.

To Whom Did Jabez Pray?

Jabez called on the God of Israel. The King of Israel; the King over all creation and all things created. He called on the Lord of Israel; the Deliverer of Israel; the Covenant God of Israel; the provider and protector of Israel; the Father of Israel; the One True and Living God! His prayer was fervent, earnest, faith-filled and humble. It is ever true that God opposes the proud and draws near to those who display humility before His throne of grace. Some scholars believe Jabez was facing enemies at the time of his prayer. His prayer then might also have been a very desperate one!

- Jesus taught us to pray to our Father in Heaven (faith) Matthew 6:9
- He taught us to ask for our daily bread (provision) Matthew 6:11
- He taught us to pray to ask forgiveness and that we would not be tempted and God would deliver us (protection/deliverance) Matthew 6:12-13

The bible teaches us that every good and perfect gift comes from God, *"Every good and perfect gift is from above, coming down from the Father of the heavenly lights, who does not change like shifting shadows." James 1:17* Now that's what I call a blessing!

What Did Jabez Pray?

Jabez asked God to bless him and to expand his territory. What does it mean to be blessed? What does expansion look like for a believer? Is it even biblical to expect God to bless us? Does God want to bless us? At this point is would seem logical to lay a Biblical foundation of our understanding of God's nature and divine will in the realm of "blessing". We cannot receive what we do not believe and we cannot believe what we have not perceived according to the word of God.

Bless

2127 eulogeo, (compound of 2093 and 3056) to speak well of, i.e. (religiously, to bless, (thank or invoke a benediction upon, prosper):- bless, praise
2128 elougetos adorable:- blessed, 3106 makarizo from 3107, to beautify i.e. pronounce (or esteem), fortunate:- call-blessed, count happy 3107 makraios supremely blest; by extens. Fortunate, well off:- blessed, happier

Origin of Blessing – The Father Heart of God for all Families

It has always been God's original intention to bless His children. Indeed the blessing of our Heavenly Father produces fruitfulness as an outflow of His presence and power operating in our lives. God's heart is to nurture and bless the family unit so that His glory may be revealed in all the earth. God is the source of all blessing and this is expressed in the cultural mandate which God gave to Adam and Eve.

"God blessed them and said to them, "Be fruitful and increase in number; fill the earth and subdue it. Rule over the fish of the sea

and the birds of the air and over every living creature that moves on the ground." Genesis 1:28

In 2 Samuel 6:20 we read how David returned to bless his household after the Ark of the Lord had been established and set in place. King David sent his people back home with a blessing and then he ensured that his own household was also blessed. David had a revelation that blessing is for all families everywhere!

God's Nature is to Bless

"I will make you into a great nation and I will bless you; I will make your name great, and you will be a blessing. I will bless those who bless you, and whoever curses you I will curse; and all peoples on earth will be blessed through you." Genesis 12:2-3

God's promise to bless Abraham and all the nations of the earth through his servant is first for the nation of Israel, the Jewish people. However, Since we the gentile church are, *"heirs together with Israel, members together of one body, and sharers together in the promise in Christ Jesus,"* (Ephesians 3:6b) we are all positioned in Christ both to receive blessing and to release blessing in the name of the Lord Jesus to the nations of the earth.

Abraham was called into a covenant relationship with God, through which God's blessing is released to all tribes and cultures. The blessing of God is not limited to our nationality; our heavenly citizenship becomes a conduit of spiritual blessing to our natural lineage regardless of our culture or nationality. Our sonship in covenant relationship with God through Christ positions us to inherit a legacy of grace blessing.

John writes, *"From the fullness of his grace we have all received one blessing after another." John 1:16* Perhaps Jabez, who was described as *"more honourable than his brothers"*, had discovered this priceless pearl and his cry to God to bless him was the result of a personal encounter with God through which he came to understand he was heir to blessing of astronomical proportion! He understood God wanted to bless him and that he had a role to place in actively participating in faith-based prayer to receive that blessing.

The Father Loves to Bless

"Come, you who are blessed by my Father; take your inheritance, the kingdom prepared for you since the creation of the world." Matthew 25:34b

Jesus spoke and demonstrated blessing, acknowledging that such blessing flows from the Father heart of God to His children. Jesus placed this blessing from His Father in the context of the Kingdom being graciously given in inheritance to the children of God. We see correlation here that those who are citizens of the Kingdom heaven are indeed heirs of blessing.

Blessing is for this life and for the life to come. *"I tell you the truth,"* Jesus replied, *"no one who has left home or brothers or sisters or mother or father or children or fields for me and the gospel will fail to receive a hundred times as much in this present age (homes, brothers, sisters, mothers, children and fields – and with them, persecutions) and in the age to come, eternal life. But many who are first will be last, and the last first."* Mark 10:29-31

The blessing of God gives us a firm faith foundation upon which we can build with the realisation that God's blessing in our lives is for a divine purpose. We are not blessed to be narcissist in reception of grace. Rather, we are blessed to be a blessing to all nations as outlined in the Abramic blessing. *"I will make you into a great nation and I will bless you; I will make your name great and you will be a blessing. I will bless those who bless you, and whoever curses you I will curse; and all peoples on earth will be blessed through you."* Genesis 12:2-3

As he prayed Jabez seems to have gained some understanding that blessing brings increase from the Lord. In the latter part of his prayer Jabez goes on to ask the Lord to enlarge his territory. In order to maintain purity of motivation such a prayer ought to flow from a life that is yielded and walking in obedience to God, so that any increase that God grants is for the furtherance of His kingdom on earth and not for selfish endeavour.

Reciprocal Blessing Flows between Heaven and Earth

Not only does God bless us, but a quick search of the Psalms reveals that they are replete with many examples of God's people ascribing greatness, glory and blessing unto His name. We see a clear principle being revealed in Scripture that blessing is reciprocal and flows between heaven and earth. God blesses His people and His people bless Him with hearts that overflow with adoration and thankfulness. We are required to engage in the process of blessing God and acknowledging on-going blessing flows from God. *"I will extol the Lord at all times; his praise will always be on my lips."* Psalm 34:1; *"For surely, O LORD, you bless the righteous; you surround them with your favour as with a shield."* Psalm 5:12

In Chapter 3 we will consider how Jesus' life was blessed and how our Saviour operated in the realm of blessing those whom He ministered with and to.

Today Lord we bless you with all of our heart, strength, soul and mind and we are grateful that we experience the blessing of God in all that we do for your glory.

In Jesus' name,
Amen

CHAPTER 3

JESUS OUR ROLE MODEL

"Blessed are the pure in heart, for they will see God."
Matthew 5:8

As we continue our reflections on the prayer of Jabez we turn to the life of our Lord Jesus to see how He moved in receiving blessing and releasing blessing. This is not an exhaustive study, but a simple overview to contextualise blessing in the New Testament in the life of Christ.

At Birth

"Then Simeon blessed them and said..." Luke 2:34

We can see evidence of blessing throughout the life and ministry of our Lord Jesus. At the time of Jesus' birth, Simeon took the Lord in his arms and blessed him, as well as also speaking a powerful blessing over Joseph and his mother Mary. The blessing of God is affirmed afresh in the New Testament context as being a blessing for the entire family and one that overflows in our lives even from the moment of our birth. The love of God our Father flows continually to us through the Son and by the Holy Spirit into every aspect of our lives and through our lives into every sphere of society in which we are graced to serve. When we speak God's blessing over our children they are propelled by grace into their destiny. The love of God creates a platform through which we can influence the lives of others.

In Ministry Blessing Releases Miracles

"Taking the five loaves and the two fish and looking up to heaven, he gave thanks and broke them. Then he gave them to the disciples to set before the people. They all ate and were satisfied, and the

disciples picked up twelve basketfuls of broken pieces that were left over."
Luke 9:16-17

When Christ multiplied the loaves and the fishes for the hungry crowds, He first blessed them by giving thanks to God and then presented them to the disciples to share amongst the people. In blessing the humble provision in the name of the Lord it miraculously multiplied into provision that was able to feed thousands. Blessing the provision we have in our hands in the name of Jesus Christ is a powerful prayer that acknowledges the omnipotence and love of our Creator God, which releases a miracle flow of our Father's abundance into our lives. Blessing and faith operate side by side. Blessing that releases miracle increase satisfies all who receive the multiplication of grace.

On more than one occasion God has blessed finances in my hands and multiplied the notes. This happened once in Uganda and one of my spiritual daughter's Rachel was witness to the multiplication. Not only did the money multiply in my hands but when I placed it into her hands it also multiplied again! It was a fantastic witness to the Muslim man who was watching the entire proceedings in the money exchange office.

As You Bless You Will Be Blessed

"But when you give a banquet, invite the poor, the crippled, the lame, the blind, and you will be blessed. Although they cannot repay you, you will be repaid at the resurrection of the righteous." Luke 14:13-14

When speaking about caring for the poor and needy, Jesus told His beloved disciples that they would be blessed as they ministered to the poor and the sick, indeed, this would be given to them as an eternal reward. It is important to realise that as we reach out in Christ's love to share the Gospel we do so from a condition of blessedness. Our witness and works of love release blessing both to those to whom we minister to and also flow back as reciprocal blessings from the Lord into our own lives. Blessing others will always bring God's increase in our own lives.

I remember once I was ministering in a park in California to the homeless people there. One lady ran off and brought back a bunch of flowers that she had found in the garbage can. They were a gift of love from her heart to mine and I was overwhelmed in the blessing of receiving them from her. They were possibly the most bedraggled bouquet I have ever seen but they meant more to me than diamonds.

Breaking Bread Releases Kingdom Blessings

"And he took bread, gave thanks and broke it, and gave it to them ..." Luke 22:19a

At the time of the Last Supper, the Lord blessed the elements of bread and wine and shared them with His disciples. The institution of the Lord's Supper was a time of Kingdom blessing at its inauguration and continues to release untold blessing to the global church as we meet in holy intimacy and union with Christ and each other.

When our Lord Jesus broke bread with the two disciples who travelled with Him on the road to Emmaus, their spiritual eyes were enlightened to comprehend and acknowledge the glory of the Risen Christ. The blessing of sharing the bread and wine is a means by which we remember Christ and His atoning death and resurrection until He returns. When we remember the victory of Calvary we stand on the firm foundation of every blessing Christ appropriated for His bride – forgiveness, healing and wholeness, righteousness, peace and joy to name but a few of the multiple blessings we have received from Christ's completed intercession on the Cross. Truly John understood this new covenant truth when he wrote, *"From the fullness of his grace we have all received one blessing after another."*

When We Praise God We Are Blessed

At the triumphal entry to Jerusalem during the time of Passover, the people of Jerusalem recognised Christ as their Messianic King. A part of their praise expression to the Lord was to shout, *"Blessed is the king who comes in the name of the Lord!" Luke 19:38a*

When we come to realise the magnitude of who Christ is and all that He has sacrificed for the salvation of mankind, we will choose to bless the Lord with all of our hearts, strength, soul and mind. Likewise, when we comprehend just how amazingly and outrageously blessed we are by God, our mouths will not be able to contain the joy we feel deep down in our souls. As we connect understanding of blessedness with crying out to God, we remember Jabez and we see a picture emerging that simultaneously convinces and perhaps also convicts us of our need to be more active in the processing of blessing. *"Oh that you would bless me indeed!"*

Even though Jesus has made a way for us to enter into blessing our mind-set can prevent us from receiving the blessing. If we do not believe God wants to bless us, or we believe we do not deserve to be blessed we will never rise up in faith to appropriate what Jesus purchased for us at the Cross. People who have suffered severe trauma and/or difficult circumstances in life can sometimes have extremely low self-esteem and suffer from feeling worthless, which can become a stumbling block to receiving blessing. God longs to heal His children in every area of brokenness and rejection so that we might step fully into His redemptive blessings.

After His Death, Resurrection and prior to the Lord's Ascension

The Risen Lord *"lifted up his hands and blessed them."* Luke 24:50

Having established that Christ's birth was marked by blessing, importantly, we also acknowledge that Jesus blessed His disciples after his death and resurrection just prior to His ascension into heaven. **The Lord's last recorded act of gracious benevolence towards His dearest disciples was to bless them**. Jesus birth, life, ministry, death, resurrection and ascension were all marked with a particular Kingdom hallmark from the Father – blessing!

This brief glimpse through the lens of both the life of Jesus' and the life of Jabez leads us to conclude that the nature of blessing is not passive. We have to actively engage in receiving and in giving blessing. As our loving Heavenly Father, God is infinitely able and eternally willing to bless His children.

Today let's open our hearts and minds afresh and remember Christ has lifted up His holy, pierced hands on the Cross to pour untold blessing upon the church. His blood sacrifice is the means by which we are blessed. It is an eternal blessing of inestimable beauty and worth.

Father, we bow our hearts and minds before you in humility and adoration; we quiet ourselves before your throne of grace and we ask today that you would enable us to be active by faith in both receiving and releasing blessing to the glory of your Name.

For Jesus' sake.
Amen

CHAPTER 4

INCREASE!

"And enlarge my territory!"

Jabez' prayer requesting blessing and increase from the Lord might be described as:

- **A prayer of breakthrough** that caused a shift in the spiritual status quo
- **A prayer of faith** that saw beyond present limitations to future opportunities
- **A prayer of trust** in the goodness of God to answer according to His will
- **A prayer of victory** to overcome difficult circumstances by the grace of God
- **A prayer of deliverance** to move from trauma and pain into healing and destiny

It is ever true that hope believes God can and faith believes God will; His love performs the deed.

The bible teaches us that God answers our prayers when we trust Him, *"They were helped in fighting them, and God handed the Hagrites and all their allies over to them, because they cried out to him during the battle. He answered their prayers, because they trusted in him."* 1 Chronicles 5:20

And our prayers to God please him, *"The LORD detests the sacrifice of the wicked, but the prayer of the upright pleases him."* Proverbs 15:8

Context: Kingdom Priority = Kingdom Blessings

What is the context of asking for God to enlarge our territory? How could a man ask God to make him bigger? Is there a Biblical blue print that we can look to? Wonderfully, the answer is a resounding YES. The Kingdom of God embodies the principle of legitimate expansion. Isaiah prophesied of Jesus Christ that, *"Of the increase of his government and peace there will be no end." Isaiah 9:7a*

Our Kingdom mandate extends unto the ends of the earth and the government of God will continue to increase throughout the earth until the return of Christ as Jesus Himself instructed His apostles, *"Therefore go and make disciples of all nations." Matthew 28:19*

Jesus teaches us to seek the increase in the context of the Kingdom of God, *"But seek first his kingdom and his righteousness, and all these things will be given to you as well." Matthew 6:33 "Ask and it will be given to you; seek and you will find; knock and the door will be opened to you. For everyone who asks receives; he who seeks finds; and to him who knocks, the door will be opened." Matthew 7:7-8*

Jesus taught us to pursue God's Kingdom before seeking anything else in our lives and as a result of giving God priority we will receive everything else we might ever need as well. **Making the Kingdom of God our primary focus is a key to unlocking untold blessings in our lives.** Those whom God blesses are blessed indeed! Blessings are real, and they have tangible effects. Jabez understood this Kingdom dynamic when he asked the Lord to increase his territory.

Whilst we do want to be active in faith concerning blessing we must also acknowledge the sovereignty of God in commanding a blessing upon His people. It is God's decision how and when and what a blessing looks like. *"I will surely bless you and make your descendants as numerous as the stars in the sky and as the sand on the seashore. Your descendants will take possession of the cities of their enemies, and through your offspring all nations on earth will be blessed, because you have obeyed me." Genesis 22:17-18*

It's important for us to note that the blessing for Abraham was connected to his obedience to God. God's magnificent promise to Abraham to bless him embraced his immediate family and the generations to come. God's blessing was spiritual (the grace and favour of God would be with and upon Abraham and his descendants always). And the blessing was also physical (Abraham's descendants would inherit entire cities as part of the blessing of God flowing in their families). God's continuous blessing through Abraham was not just for his own family for but all families all over the world. God's blessings release His Kingdom here on earth!

In Africa during rainy season the rain falls at a tremendous rate and can quickly wash away roads, cause trees to be swept away and will swiftly move anything in its path. Ezekiel teaches us that rain showers are symbolic of blessing, *"I will bless them and the places surrounding my hill. I will send down showers in season; there will be showers of blessing." Ezekiel 34:26*
May I suggest we need a mind-set change to receive blessing like Ezekiel describes, as a deluge of rain that can wash away disappointment, delay and disaster and usher us into phenomenal harvest blessings from God.

We need God to enlarge our hearts and increase our portion *of Him* so that we might become even more fruitful *in Him*. When we pray and ask God to expand our territory we believe that He will prosper our endeavours whether for ministry or family, for work or for warfare.

When we posture ourselves to pray for increase it means we most likely already have a testimony of the constancy of God in our own lives. Our personal testimony of God's goodness and faithfulness becomes a foundation from which He can elevate our prayer lives to a new level of breakthrough. It is impossible not to praise God when we experience His goodness. A lifestyle of praise and faith-fuelled prayer can only result in a believer being better equipped and empowered to serve God.

Asking God to enlarge our territory, when we ask out of adoration and God reliance releases the limitless power, authority and love of God. Increase speaks of more favour, more wealth, more joy, more grace, more of everything of the blessings God has for our lives. Increase ushers us into new divine opportunities and open doors. Our Heavenly Father is an extravagant God! *"How great is the love the Father has lavished on us, that we should be called children of God! And that is what we are!" 1 John 3:1a*

Asking God for increase is not a selfish prayer so long as the motivation of that prayer is about seeing God glorified and His Kingdom advance rather than looking for personal glorification or reward. Understanding that God wants to use us/His church to be agents of transformation to people, situations and nations will cause our prayer life to be radically changed and reshaped. We will begin to intercede from a desire for enlargement in God and for God and to make a greater impact for Him. This type of prayer for expansion will become our new paradigm. It will cause a shift in us that will usher us into greater blessing to experience the overflow of heaven in our own lives and to help others to enter into amplified Kingdom blessings in their lives too. A prayer of proliferation from a pure heart will manifest the heart and will of God in every situation.

When we enter into the realm of increase and acceleration in our ministries by the grace of God, there are a few basic principles we need to understand:

Provision
We shift from dreaming with God of the impossible, to walking with God in what has been made possible by His grace. When we see with eyes of faith the dream-able becomes do-able when God is our focus and our best hope, *"For nothing is impossible with God." Luke 1:37*

We move from ambivalence to awakening and believing to receiving just as the Israelites moved from the faith position of eating manna every day to eating of the fruit of the Promised Land.

Simeon dreamt of holding Christ but then came the day of God's fulfilment of blessing and Simeon's dream became a reality as he held Christ in his own arms and prophesied. *"Sovereign Lord, as you have promised, you now dismiss your servant in peace. For my eyes have seen your salvation, which you have prepared in the sight of all people, a light for revelation to the Gentiles and for glory to your people Israel." Luke 2:29-32*

We move from dreaming to doing and from being a Kingdom visionary with hope to being a Kingdom implementer with divine purpose. Such a shift will create a new paradigm of restoration out of the ashes of devastation. Nehemiah had a dream to rebuild the broken down wall and the burned gates of Jerusalem. There is a time in God to dream and a time in God to do. When the Kairos timing of God brought about a shift, Nehemiah knew it was time to build. He shared his vison and people came on board because it was the season for increase and enlargement. The same principles apply for us today.

Stepping into new faith arenas will stretch our faith. We cannot prepare for what lies ahead in the future by relying on whatever qualifications we have gained or on any training or experience we have accumulated thus far. As valuable as these things may be it is only the grace of God that will sustain us in the faith space that the prayer of "enlarge my territory" occupies. It is not our past experiences, our finances, our status, the people we know or the gifting God has placed within us that will carry us into the momentum of multiplication. It is the provision of God our faithful Father that will enable us to fulfil new mandates and missions. His supply will sustain us in new frontiers of spiritual and physical expansion.

God will send His angels to help us; He will gift us with the Holy Spirit, and with wisdom, discernment, courage and faith. He will speak to us through Scripture. We will grow into the increase by staying God-reliant and humble. The prayer of Jabez for "enlargement" begins with acknowledging our need to decrease so that God might increase in us. Before God enlarges our territory He gives us the grace to decrease, which diminishes our ability to be self-sufficient in order that He might increase our capacity to be God-reliant. In the place of faith expansion our opportunities far outweigh and overtake any capability that has brought us this far. God provides all that we need out of the abundance of His grace. He teaches us how to pray for His will to be done.

People

At every destiny milestone God will put people in our path that will become the means by which He will unlock our destiny. It has been my experience that when God opens up new vistas on a spiritual journey He will introduce others who are also people who are seeking spiritual enlargement for the glory of God. These God-ordained relationships become strategic connections from which Kingdom alliances are outworked as we interact with others in the body of Christ and in society. Cherish and honour the relationships you have in your life. Look for opportunities to bless others and do not miss the blessing God has for you through them.

Spheres

Jesus taught, *"And the gospel of the kingdom will be preached in the whole world as a testimony to all nations, and then the end will come." Matthew 24:14*

When God enlarges our territory, the Kingdom of God expands in every geographical location and in every sphere of society including government, church, family, media, arts, education and business. We were created for impact and to positively influence and transform every place where we have been given favour to serve God. Increase brings with it responsibilities and challenges as well as blessings but it is ever true that with the gift of "call" comes the grace to walk in it and all that it encompasses.

"Enlarge my territory" isn't a place where our training or past experience can take us although they may serve as a foundation for any new work God is doing in and through our lives. It is only out of the abundance of being enlarged by God's grace that we gain the experience we do not have to fulfil Kingdom assignments set before us. To ask God to enlarge our territory is another way of saying, "Lord, I surrender my life to you and I trust you to lead me in your will. I believe you will sustain me where you lead me and you will provide for that which your will desires. Lord, enlarge my territory and enable me to have increased ministry opportunities to bring glory to you and advance Your Kingdom here on earth! Use me as an agent of transformation."

God teaches us how to manage the resource He has entrusted to our hands. Stewardship is the gift of wisdom and compassion in administration of God-given resource for the purpose for which God intended it to be used ….. To bless and be a blessing!

Father, enable us to have the faith to ask You for increase and to have the trust in You that You will teach us how to manage that increase with diligence and grace,

In Jesus' name,
Amen

CHAPTER 5

GIVE ME YOUR HAND

"Let your hand be with me,
And keep me from harm
So that I will be free from pain."

Jabez asked for the Lord's hand to be with him. The hand of God is a biblical term for God's power and presence in the lives of His people. God did the seemingly impossible and dried up the Jordan River to allow the Israelites to cross over and the Bible records this as a demonstration of His miracle-working power, *"He did this so that all the peoples of the earth might know that the hand of the LORD is powerful and so that you might always fear the LORD your God." Joshua 4:24*

Like Jabez as we pray for enlargement it will often bring us to a milestone in our faith journey and we may look at giant obstacles and impossibilities and wonder if we can ever summon the faith to overcome them. The miracle of the Jordan drying up can help to wash away those doubts!

There are times in our walk with God when we reach a crossroads and we need to springboard from the past and dive into the new things God has for us. It can be a somewhat daunting prospect but how wonderful to know that we can rely on the power of God's hand to usher us into the next stage of the fulfilment of His dreams for our lives.

The prophet Isaiah clearly understood that God was able and willing to protect and deliver His people. Isaiah wrote that God's arm was able to save His people. *"Surely the arm of the LORD is not too short to save, nor his ear too dull to hear." Isaiah 59:1*

When we are shifting from one level to another new level and our faith is being stretched it can be a time of wondering, "Does God really hear?" Isaiah's words were a comfort to the people of God thousands of years ago and they still edify and encourage us today. The same God of Abraham, Isaac and Jacob is listening for our prayers desirous to save us from the snare of the enemy and deliver us from the dominion of darkness into the Kingdom of the Son whom He loves. Whether you feel like a grasshopper or a giant slayer, God is forever faithful and He is always a great and mighty God. God is a giant slayer.

Incredibly, the Scriptures record that God is waiting and watching, longing to pour out the blessing of His strength in our lives. God wants to answer our prayers of increase. *"For the eyes of the LORD range throughout the earth to strengthen those whose hearts are fully committed to him." 2 Chronicles 16:9*

Apostle Paul spoke words of deep wisdom and insight when he wrote to the church in Ephesus that God's strength was sufficient for him in his time of weakness. There may times when we are not always strong in our faith walk; may I suggest that by permitting us to experience moments of personal weakness that this could be God's way of helping us to walk in humility? As we trust and obey the Lord we can always rely on His unfailing strength to propel us in the momentum of grace, ever forward as men and women of faith, hope and love.

The hand of God guides and directs us in our time of need. We receive provision and are equipped and empowered. The hand of God is associated with the righteous judgement of God upon His enemies as well as justice for the poor and oppressed, *"Blessed are they who maintain justice, who constantly do what is right." Psalm 106:3*

The New Testament is replete with examples of the blessing of God's hand upon His people. God granted favour and success to the early apostolic church, *"The Lord's hand was with them, and a great number of people believed and turned to the Lord."* Acts 11:21 The blessings we receive from God are so huge that they have the potential to overflow into the lives of many others, just as we see in the early New Testament Church. God blessed His people and the blessing resulted in a harvest of souls, with disciples being nurtured and the church growing in numbers and in strength. Blessing from God has a corporate application as much as it has a personal one. God's hand works in us, for us and through us and His hand is all-sufficient for our needs.

As New Testament believers today the Holy Spirit enables us to experience the hand of the Lord in our lives.

Jesus' hands were pierced on Calvary's Cross so that we might experience forgiveness, redemption, healing and wholeness. The hands of God in Christ represent His victory and authority and power over sin, death, the devil and every kind of sickness and disease. The hands of Jesus flow with compassion to heal the sick, deliver the demonised, raise the dead, cleanse the leper and bring hope and healing to all.

The Great Commission is an amazing blessing and yet it is also a seemingly unachievable task. Nonetheless, God's hand releases His power through His church to accomplish His will and bring Him glory despite what may seem impossibility to us. It is quite simple: the plans of God need the hands of God and what the Lord commissions He will also bring to completion.

Keep Me from Evil

Jabez prayed with understanding; he knew his sin had the potential to cause much pain to others as well as to himself. Jabez didn't pray for God to deliver him from temptation, he prayed that God would keep him away from evil in the first place. Hindsight is a wonderful thing: character is much easier kept than it is recovered.

Without a doubt, success is accompanied by great opportunities either for success or for failure and the devil understands that; more importantly so does God, which is why Jesus taught us to pray, *"And lead us not into temptation, but deliver us from the evil one." Matthew 6:13*

Jabez' prayer to be kept from evil is a pre-emptive prayer full of divinely inspired wisdom. It is a prayer of relational surrender and absolute belief in God's ability to lead us in paths of righteousness for His namesake. In other words away from trouble and out of temptation!

Jabez already knew what pain was and he prayed for God to keep him from any further harm. Who wants more pain when you can ask God for more blessing!

Heavenly Father, we receive your hand of blessing in our lives and we bless your holy name as you keep us from evil as we serve you.

In Jesus' name,
Amen

CHAPTER 6

SUCCESS!

"And God granted his request."

Let's remind ourselves of Jabez' simple, yet extraordinary prayer of audacious faith.

"Jabez cried out to the God of Israel,
Oh, that you would bless me
And enlarge my territory!
Let your hand be with me,
And keep me from harm
So that I will be free from pain."
And God granted his request."
1 Chronicles 4:10

The Success of his Prayer

Prosperity, protection and blessing came to Jabez in remarkable abundance and God gave him success IN ALL! The Lord answered his prayer and gave Jabez what he had requested – blessing and increase through the anointing of the Holy Spirit. We can reasonably assume this was both a source of spiritual and also physical blessing and one that had both personal and corporate effects. It was a blessing to Jabez, to his family and all other lives that he was privileged to connect with and have influence over. Jabez' uncomplicated and simple prayer released profusion and plenty from God. The favour of God was on him and God blessed him extravagantly.

Historically, it is good to remind ourselves that the post-exilic community core tribes were Judah, Levi and Benjamin. Jabez is believed to be of the tribe of Judah. When we consider King David's ancestral heritage and the continuity of this line through the exile and beyond, God's blessing on Jabez was even more remarkable. The divine granting of land would have been extremely important in a post-exilic community.

Jesus Teaches the Principle of More Than

Jesus taught His disciples how to emulate Him in character, in mission and in ministry. Astonishingly, the Lord said that we would do even greater miracles that He had done during his earthly ministry. In order to enter into the "greater things" Jesus' spoke of we need to comprehend that the answer to such prayer is focused on the expansion of the Kingdom of God here on earth. Jesus teaches us that God wants to bless us more than we can ask or imagine.

"I tell you the truth, anyone who has faith in me will do what I have been doing. He will do even greater things than these, because I am going to the Father. And I will do whatever you ask in my name, so that the Son may bring glory to the Father. You may ask me for anything in my name, and I will do it." John 14:12-14
"If you remain in me and my words remain in you, ask whatever you wish, and it will be given you." John 15:7

God has not only given us a Biblical testimony in Jabez' life of how he wants to bless us; He has also given us a clear Biblical imperative to believe and pray for increase through what Jesus taught and demonstrated in His ministry of miracles, signs, wonders and salvations.

In summarising, let's remind ourselves of some of the main principles of God's blessings:

The origin of blessing flows from the Father heart of God for all families in every nation, in all time (Genesis 1:28; Acts 2:38-39)

God's nature is to bless those who are in covenant relationship with Him (Genesis 12:2-3)

Our Heavenly Father loves to bless us with a Kingdom inheritance (Matthew 25:34b)

Jesus grace' is so full that we have received the potential of endless blessings (John 1:16)

Blessings *from God* are intimately woven into our obedience *to God* (Genesis 22:18)

Blessings are for this life and also for the life to come (Mark 10:29-31)

Reciprocal blessings flow between heaven and earth (Psalm 5:12; 34:1)

Jesus Himself received blessings (Luke 2:34)

Blessing releases God's miracles to us (Luke 9:16-17)

As you bless others, you will be blessed (Luke 14:13-14)

Breaking bread and a close relationship with God ushers us into abundant blessing (Luke 22:19a)

When we praise God we are blessed. As we sow to the heavens, He sows to the earth and uses our lives as a point of contact for releasing miracle blessings (Luke 19:38)

Jesus blessed others; He was up close and personal in blessing people (Luke 24:50)

God is sovereign as to how and when He blesses us (Genesis 22:17-18)

God promises to shower us with blessings. Prepare for a destiny deluge of blessing! (Ezekiel 34:26)

God is a lavish Father who loves to extravagantly bless His children (1 John 3:1a)

The context of praying for increase and blessing needs to flow from a Kingdom focus and priority (Matthew 7:6-8)
Blessing is a New Testament Kingdom principle. God wants to bless the earth through His church (Matthew 28:19)

It's clear that there is a Biblical mandate for asking God to bless us! As we ask the Lord to bless us He releases healing, wholeness, breakthrough and victory to overcome any and all situations.

Praying for blessing releases the miracle-working power of God in, to and through our lives. Of course we recognise it is more blessed to give than to receive and as God blesses us we are blessed to be a blessing!

Top Tips

- Own the prayer! Pray it for yourself and for your family/friends, your ministry and your career and in every area in which you are seeking breakthrough, blessing and increase.

- Ask God to bless you! Jabez did and he was magnificently and outrageously blessed by God.

- Pray with the assurance that God is the source of all blessing. His blessings are beautiful and bounteous and free!

- God is willing and able to bless all His children – He simply cannot and never will run out of blessings; His blessings are consistent and He is faithful.

- Blessings are not related to our goodness, but to God's goodness.

- God wants to bless you far more than you know how to ask or receive it.

- Ask the Lord to give you faith to pray for increase; God wants to expand His kingdom through you and your family, your church and every sphere in which you are His ambassador.

- Pray knowing that you are entering into a cycle of blessing for you and your entire family, for your children and your children's children. Blessing is generational!

- Expect to receive blessing both spiritually and physically. God promised to bless Abraham and his descendants with both physical and spiritual blessings. You are praying from a Biblical faith foundation when you ask God to bless you.

- Ask God to bless you through His provision and also to bless you in His mighty strength and protection over your life.

- Determine to enter into the fullness of blessing because in Christ we can receive one blessing after another.

- Trust God to know how and when to pour out His blessing in your life. He has heard your prayer and He will answer according to His perfect will.

- Don't give up if the blessing is delayed – God's timing is perfect. Delay is not denial and your blessing is on the way! Keep seeing with eyes of faith.

- Accept the favour of God as a continuous blessing on your life that will open multiple doors of blessing and influence for you.

- Receive the anointing from the Holy Spirit to both discern and walk in the increase of all God's blessings in your life.

- Walk in humility and love as you experience miracle blessing and breakthrough.

As Jabez prayed to the God of Israel so we now also pray with great faith,

"Oh, that you would bless me
And enlarge my territory!
Let your hand be with me,
And keep me from harm
So that I will be free from pain."
And God granted his request."

In Jesus' all powerful name, Amen.

God bless you! You are a world changer and a history maker for the glory of God!

ABOUT CATHERINE

Catherine Brown is the Founder and International Director of Gatekeepers Global Ministries (GGM) and Gatekeepers Global Leadership Network (GGLN). She is a sought-after national and international preacher and teacher. She has spent the last 7 years leading a global evangelism and discipleship mission entitled "GGM 7 Million Souls" and now continues to work with her team and valued partners in building the Kingdom of God in 34+ nations/regions.

Catherine lives on the West coast of Scotland with her husband and together they have four grown up children.

www.gatekeepers.org.uk
Admin@gatekeepers.org.uk

OTHER BOOKS BY CATHERINE BROWN

(All available worldwide via Amazon)

SIMPLY APOSTOLIC (3 VOLUME SET)

"Simply Apostolic" is an eye-opener into the often controversial world of apostolic ministry. Catherine Brown has written fearlessly and comprehensively on the topic of authentic apostolic ministry, bringing cutting edge insight into the gift and function of apostles and apostolic ministry in the 21st century church. Respected senior Christian leaders from around the world have endorsed this daring and controversial book. Throughout, it clearly
outlines valuable authentic Kingdom principles and practical protocols on apostolic functionality, and takes the reader on an amazing behind-the-scenes journey to understand what it means to be a "sent one". This book is a profound combination of courageous articulation of biblical truth, sound doctrine, wisdom and practical experience written in a clear, concise, practical and unpretentious style. For those interested in advancing the Kingdom of God and understanding more about apostolic leadership, this volume will deliver priceless knowledge and insight.

Paperback ISBN's
Volume 1 – 9781909805064; Volume 2 – 9781909805040;
Volume 3 – 9781909805095
eBook ISBN's Volume 1 – 9781909805101;
Volume 2 – 9781909805118; Volume 3 - 9781909805125

KINGDOM BUILDING – REALISING VISION AND DEVELOPING LEADERS

This book seeks to envision emerging leaders and also equips existing leaders to step out in bold Kingdom ventures. Catherine's latest book is a must read for all established visionary leaders and for those who are emerging as aspiring leaders. It is full of wisdom and solid biblical teaching. Catherine draws from her own ministry experience in leading global vision and does so in a transparent and straightforward fashion. The topics in the books include how to recognise your season in the Lord, how to conceive, consolidate and build foundations for vision. How to be prepared to carry vision, how to implement, share and lead vision to completion. Advice on partnership, vision, values, balance in leadership, investing in team, setting goals, dealing with enemy opposition and obtaining counter strategy and much, much more.

"This is a wonderfully practical book that melds together Godly values with our best efforts to bring forth Kingdom strategy. It challenges us to lay a true foundation for realizing vision by nurturing the right heart attitude with God and our fellow ministry partners. Then it builds on that solid foundation with straightforward and accessible principles and guidelines. May visions be realized; May leaders be developed; May God's Kingdom Come."
Rev. Wesley Zinn, Wellspring Church

ISBN's Paperback 9781909805149; ebook 9781909805071

ENCOUNTER – LESSONS IN CHRISTIAN LEADERSHIP (VOLUMES 1-3)

The *"Encounter – Lessons in Christian Leadership"* series written by Catherine Brown is a succession of life study booklets on some of the great leaders of both the Old Testament and the New Testament, which focus on Kingdom leadership principles and practical applications of spiritual truths. In addition to sound Scriptural teaching, Catherine also shares from her own extensive personal experience as a Christian leader. Over the last 15 years she has worked alongside many churches and ministries in varying capacities including overseeing churches and ministries; developing and outworking strategy/vision at local, national and international levels for prayer, worship, evangelism, church planting and discipleship as well as leadership development in church and conference settings and in the market place. This series has already received excellent feedback from Church leaders, who have been encouraged and strengthened through reading. The first volume in the series, *"Mobilisation and Management – A Study in the Life of Moses"* is a succinct creative analysis in the life of an inspirational leader of the Christian faith: Moses, a servant leader with a Kingdom mission and mind-set. Volume two of the Encounter series focuses on the life and trials of Joseph as an apostolic leader for the nation of Israel.

Paperback ISBN's: Volume 1 – 9781909805194; Volume 2 – 9781909805200
EBook ISBN's: Volume 1 – 9780956208668; Volume 2 – 9781909805118

THE STORY OF LEAH (OVERCOMING REJECTION)

The courage and tenacity of Leah in the midst of extremely difficult circumstances have spoken profoundly to Catherine on overcoming rejection. Leah is a powerful testimony as to how a person can choose to overcome rejection and trust in God's faithfulness and grace to carry them beyond defeat, into a time of refreshing and personal renewal and restoration. This short volume will inspire and delight the reader as the author comprehensively addresses the issues surrounding rejection by winding her own personal experiences through the rich biblical tapestry of the story of Leah. Practical notes are included on how to recognize rejection and how to pray for healing from its debilitating effects

Paperback ISBN 9781909805293; ebook 9781909805286

AN INSPIRATIONAL MONTH

"An Inspirational Month for Christian Leaders" will encourage, inspire and bless busy leaders from all walks of life. Catherine has woven together a unique tapestry of faith inspired contemporary and historical spiritual quotes, motivational thoughts and Bible verses along with a short thought-provoking commentary for each of the 31 day entries on topics pertinent to leaders who are also disciplers. She has included a space for reader's reflection. "A dream without a team cannot succeed; a team without a dream can, however, fail." Catherine writes, "I have discovered that the strategic nature of Christian leadership is to love selflessly beyond fear or betrayal; see Kingdom potential beyond pitfalls; value the DNA of family beyond a programme; invest in others and build teams; model radical faith; be focused in thought; intentional in action; inspirational in speech; consistent in communication; collaborative in relationships; wise with resource; constant in prayer; fruitful in outcomes and exemplary in character by the grace of God."

Paperback ISBN 9781909805255
E-book 9781909805262

TO ISRAEL WITH LOVE

The message in **To Israel with Love** will help the reader break free from hatred, indifference and ignorance as they discover the eternal truth about God's love and covenant with the Jewish people. *"Catherine has truly captured the Father's heart for Israel and the Jewish people through a mother's eyes. The prophetic insight is as new wine for a new day!"*

Curt Landry, House of David Ministries
Catherine Brown has written a book laced with prophetic spirit. She interweaves prophetic visions, solid Scriptural exposition and words directly from King Abba's heart. The resulting balance is simultaneously alive, encouraging and refreshing. Catherine, like Ruth of old, has found rest and prophetic refreshment under the shade of Israel's olive tree, and the blessing
on her words is proof positive of her blessing of Israel. The prophetic sap of God's ancient olive tree runs through this book. Enjoy!"

Avner Boskey, David's Tent www.davidstent.org

Currently only available as an eBook ISBN 9780956208651

MIRACLES AND MAYHEM – THE MINISTRY OF FAMILIES

Miracles and Mayhem charts God's heart for families and the biblical foundation for family life and is a compelling account of a family's every day journey together in the Kingdom of God.

"Don't buy this book if you want a God that is safe, predictable and cosily locked up in a box only to be opened on Sundays. Don't buy this book if you want to feel safe in your daily life from a God who invades the ordinary and makes it extraordinary. However, do buy it if you long for the reality of a God who can come into the chaos of family life and speak to you through ordinary everyday incidents. If you want a God who talks to ordinary people and shows them extraordinary things and uses them to touch a hurting world with healing grace, then do buy this book. You won't regret it."
Rev Eric Delve, Chairman of Revival Fire Conferences

"Catherine's book is heart-warming. You will be challenged, touched and encouraged as you read about her family. You will be blessed as you enjoy Catherine and Stephen's journey, and spiritual insight."
Dr. Heidi Baker, Director Iris Ministries

ISBN's Paperback 9788190249164; eBook 9780956208620

CONFESSIONS OF A FASTING HOUSEWIFE
(ONE WOMAN'S JOURNEY WITH JESUS)

Confessions of a Fasting Housewife is an open and honest diary of Catherine's attempt to fast for 40 days and serves as a guide to anyone considering a fast whether short or extended. This book is described as, *"more than a spiritual guide to fasting - it is a practical primer on the "dos and don'ts" of fasting.* As you read Catherine Brown's experiences, you will find yourself empathising, and at times, outright laughing at her candid confessions of the emotional ups and downs involved with fasting in the 21st century. Spirituality and practicality meet head-on in *Confessions of a Fasting Housewife*. Get ready to learn everything your pastor never told you about fasting! Then ... fast!

Victoria Boyson writer of the foreword states, *"Confessions of a Fasting Housewife is a masterpiece of mercy and will open up your heart and mind to receive the grace to love God more than ever."*

Currently only available as a paperback ISBN: Paperback 9788889127100

THE NORMAL, THE DEEP AND THE CRAZY
(Catherine's Testimony)
Available in English, French and Spanish

The Normal, the Deep and the Crazy, is a transparent and moving account of Catherine's life with a violent and alcoholic father, her illegitimacy and her healing testimony since she found the Lord. The book is written in an amazingly transparent style and has been described as "*A light for your journey, a hope for your heart and a mission for your life.*"

James Goll writer of the foreword says, "*With a whole heart I gladly endorse the contents of this inspiring book. I trust it will do for you, what it did for me. I found myself more in love with our Father God who desires to see restoration happen in the lives of countless warriors-in-waiting.*"

Paperback ISBN's English – 9780956208606; French – 9782952367097;
EBook ISBN's English – 9781909805002; Spanish - 9780956208613

.

67965136R00027

Made in the USA
Charleston, SC
01 March 2017